Stevenson

by Iain Gray

GW00391872

Lang**Syne**

PUBLISHING

WRITING *to* REMEMBER

Lang**Syne**

PUBLISHING

WRITING *to* REMEMBER

79 Main Street, Newtongrange,
Midlothian EH22 4NA
Tel: 0131 344 0414   Fax: 0845 075 6085
E-mail: info@lang-syne.co.uk
www.langsyneshop.co.uk

Design by Dorothy Meikle
Printed by Printwell Ltd
© Lang Syne Publishers Ltd 2016

ISBN 978-1-85217-369-2

Stevenson

MOTTO:
Peace in freedom
(and)
Rest under liberty.

CREST:
A golden wheat sheaf.

NAME variations include:
Steanson
Steenson
Stenson
Stephansan
Stephensen
Stephenson
Stimson
Stinson
Steen

Echoes of a far distant past
can still be found in most names

Chapter one:

Origins of Scottish surnames

by George Forbes

It all began with the Normans.

For it was they who introduced surnames into common usage more than a thousand years ago, initially based on the title of their estates, local villages and chateaux in France to distinguish and identify these landholdings, usually acquired at the point of a bloodstained sword.

Such grand descriptions also helped enhance the prestige of these arrogant warlords and generally glorify their lofty positions high above the humble serfs slaving away below in the pecking order who only had single names, often with Biblical connotations as in Pierre and Jacques.

The only descriptive distinctions among this peasantry concerned their occupations, like Pierre the swineherd or Jacques the ferryman.

The Normans themselves were originally Vikings (or Northmen) who raided, colonised and eventually settled down around the French coastline.

They had sailed up the Seine in their longboats in 900 AD under their ferocious leader Rollo and ruled the roost in north east France before sailing over to conquer England, bringing their relatively new tradition of having surnames with them.

It took another hundred years for the Normans to percolate northwards and surnames did not begin to appear in Scotland until the thirteenth century.

These adventurous knights brought an aura of chivalry with them and it was said no damsel of any distinction would marry a man unless he had at least two names.

The family names included that of Scotland's great hero Robert De Brus and his compatriots were warriors from families like the De Morevils, De Umphravils, De Berkelais, De Quincis, De Viponts and De Vaux.

As the knights settled the boundaries of their vast estates, they took territorial names, as in Hamilton, Moray, Crawford, Cunningham, Dunbar, Ross, Wemyss, Dundas, Galloway, Renfrew, Greenhill, Hazelwood, Sandylands and Church-hill.

Other names, though not with any obvious geographical or topographical features, nevertheless derived from ancient parishes like Douglas, Forbes, Dalyell and Guthrie.

Other surnames were coined in connection with occupations, castles or legendary deeds. Stuart originated in the word steward, a prestigious post which was an integral part of any large medieval household. The same applied to Cooks, Chamberlains, Constables and Porters.

Borders towns and forts – needed in areas like the Debateable Lands which were constantly fought over by feuding local families – had their own distinctive names; and it was often from them that the resident groups took their communal titles, as in the Grahams of Annandale, the Elliots and Armstrongs of the East Marches, the Scotts and Kerrs of Teviotdale and Eskdale.

Even physical attributes crept into surnames, as in Small, Little and More (the latter being 'beg' in Gaelic), Long or Lang, Stark, Stout, Strong or Strang and even Jolly.

Mieklejohns would have had the strength of several men, while Littlejohn was named after the legendary sidekick of Robin Hood.

Colours got into the act with Black, White, Grey, Brown and Green (Red developed into Reid,

Ruddy or Ruddiman). Blue was rare and nobody ever wanted to be associated with yellow.

Pompous worthies took the name Wiseman, Goodman and Goodall.

Words intimating the sons of leading figures were soon affiliated into the language as in Johnson, Adamson, Richardson and Thomson, while the Norman equivalent of Fitz (from the French-Latin 'filius' meaning 'son') cropped up in Fitzmaurice and Fitzgerald.

The prefix 'Mac' was 'son of' in Gaelic and clans often originated with occupations – as in MacNab being sons of the Abbot, MacPherson and MacVicar being sons of the minister and MacIntosh being sons of the chief.

The church's influence could be found in the names Kirk, Clerk, Clarke, Bishop, Friar and Monk. Proctor came from a church official, Singer and Sangster from choristers, Gilchrist and Gillies from Christ's servant, Mitchell, Gilmory and Gilmour from servants of St Michael and Mary, Malcolm from a servant of Columba and Gillespie from a bishop's servant.

The rudimentary medical profession was represented by Barber (a trade which also once included dentistry and surgery) as well as Leech or Leitch.

Businessmen produced Merchants, Mercers, Monypennies, Chapmans, Sellers and Scales, while down at the old village watermill the names that cropped up included Miller, Walker and Fuller.

Other self explanatory trades included Coopers, Brands, Barkers, Tanners, Skinners, Brewsters and Brewers, Tailors, Saddlers, Wrights, Cartwrights, Smiths, Harpers, Joiners, Sawyers, Masons and Plumbers.

Even the scenery was utilised as in Craig, Moor, Hill, Glen, Wood and Forrest.

Rank, whether high or low, took its place with Laird, Barron, Knight, Tennant, Farmer, Husband, Granger, Grieve, Shepherd, Shearer and Fletcher.

The hunt and the chase supplied Hunter, Falconer, Fowler, Fox, Forrester, Archer and Spearman.

The renowned medieval historian Froissart, who eulogised about the romantic deeds of chivalry (and who condemned Scotland as being a poverty stricken wasteland), once sniffily dismissed the peasantry of his native France as the jacquerie (or the

jacques-without-names) but it was these same
humble folk who ended up overthrowing the arrogant
aristocracy.

In the olden days, only the blueblooded
knights of antiquity were entitled to full, proper names,
both Christian and surnames, but with the passing of
time and a more egalitarian, less feudal atmosphere,
more respectful and worthy titles spread throughout
the populace as a whole.

Echoes of a far distant past can still be found
in most names and they can be borne with pride in
commemoration of past generations who fought and
toiled in some capacity or other to make our nation
what it now is, for good or ill.

Chapter two:

Saints and sinners

**Derived from the Greek word 'stephanos', mean-
ing 'garland', 'crown' or 'wreath', the Stevenson
name has been prevalent throughout the length
and breadth of Scotland from earliest times.**

The 'Stevenson' form is almost unique to
Scotland, while the 'Stephenson' form is more
popular south of the Border – but what both have in
common is that, denoting 'son of Steven', or 'son of
Stephen', they honour St Stephen.

Recognised as the first Christian martyr after
Christ, the saint was stoned to death by a furious mob
around 34-35 A.D. after being deemed guilty of
blasphemy by the priests of the Temple in Jerusalem.

Commonly depicted with a crown, denoting
martyrdom for Christianity, he is venerated as a
saint by the Anglican, Roman Catholic, Eastern
Orthodox and Lutheran churches, while his feast
day is December 26 – popularly recognised by
Western Christians as St Stephen's Day, or the Feast
of Stephen.

Some sources assert that the Stevenson name

and its rather bewildering number of variations were first introduced to British shores in the wake of the Norman Conquest of 1066, but there is also evidence that the names may have become established some time before this.

A family of the name are believed to have been firmly settled before the eleventh century Norman invasion in Northumberland, in the north of England, with wealthy landholdings in the area of present-day Newcastle-upon-Tyne, and with a family seat at Knaresdale Hall.

By the mid-12th century, a branch of the family settled in the Scottish Borders in the parish of Newlands, near Peebles, and it is from here that we find a Stevene Stevenson recorded on the infamous Ragman Roll of 1296.

It was in July of that year that the Scots rose in armed revolt against the imperialist designs of the English king Edward I, but, living up to his reputation of 'Hammer of the Scots', he brought the entire nation under his subjugation little less than a month later.

To reinforce his domination of the blighted Scottish nation, 1,500 earls, bishops and burgesses such as Stevene Stevenson were required to sign a humiliating treaty of fealty, known as the Ragman

Roll, because of the number of ribbons that dangled from the seals of the reluctant signatories.

There are also records of a John Steywynson in Banff, in the north of Scotland, in 1388, a John Stevin in Aberdeen in the early years of the 16th century and an Alexander Stevyn recorded at the same period in Glasgow.

The name is also found today in the ancient Irish province of Ulster, mainly in the forms of 'Steenson' and 'Stinson' – with bearers of the name descendants of those Scots who were 'planted' there in the early years of the 17th century.

This policy of Plantation involved the settlement of Scottish Protestants on land that had been held for centuries by those native Catholic Irish considered rebellious by the omnipotent British Crown.

In later centuries, many of these Scots-Irish were forced through dire circumstance, not least the terrible 19th century Great Famine, to establish new lives for themselves in North America, Australia and New Zealand – and where their proud descendants thrive to this day.

Although found from earliest times throughout Scotland, it was in the wild Border lands that bearers of the Stevenson name lived a particularly lawless life, in common with other Border clans such as the Elliots, Douglases, Homes, Swintons, Armstrongs, Maxwells, Johnstones and Grahams.

It was in an attempt to bring order to what was known as the 'debateable land' on both sides of the Border, that Alexander II of Scotland in 1237 signed the Treaty of York, which for the first time established the Scottish border with England as a line running from the Solway to the Tweed.

Under Border Law, complaints from either side of the Border were dealt with on Truce Days, while there was also a law known as the Hot Trod, that granted anyone who had their livestock stolen the right to pursue the thieves and recover their property within a certain time limit.

But this was not enough to curb what had become a state of near anarchy.

In 1603, James VI, after acceding to the throne of England as James I, attempted to solve the problem once and for all by abolishing Border Law and even the very name of 'Borders', in favour of 'Middle Shires.'

But, five years later, matters were still so bad that a Scottish Privy Council report graphically noted how the 'wild incests, adulteries, convocation of the lieges, shooting and wearing of hackbuts, pistols, lances, daily bloodshed, oppression, and disobedience in civil matters, neither are nor has been punished.'

What eventually brought relative peace to the Borders was the settlement in the early years of the seventeenth century of troublesome Border clans such as the Stevensons in Ulster, as already noted.

From the Borders to the western seaboard of Scotland, Stevensons also established a close bond of kinship with the proud Clan MacTavish, whose seat was at Dunardary, near the western end of the Crinan Canal, in Argyll.

Along with clans that include those of Cash, MacLehose, MacThomas, Thom, Thompson and Todd, the Stevensons/Stephensons are recognised as a sept of Clan MacTavish – whose motto is 'Not forgetful' and whose crest is a boar's head.

As a recognised branch of the MacTavishes and, accordingly, entitled to wear their clan tartan, the Stevensons of Argyll shared in both the clan's fortunes and misfortunes.

These tragic misfortunes most memorably included Flodden, in September of 1513, when Ewin MacTavish and a number of his Stevenson kinsfolk were among the estimated 10,000 Scots killed in battle against the English.

Nearly 235 years later, in April of 1746, MacTavishes and their kinsfolk were among those Jacobites slain at the equally disastrous battle of Culloden.

Chapter three:

All in the family

Far from the destructive field of battle, generations of bearers of the Stevenson name and its variations have made a decidedly more positive and enduring contribution to society – in the form of legacies that survive to this day.

This is not least through a truly remarkable dynasty of pioneering Scottish civil engineers and literary figures.

The 'father' of this particular Stevenson dynasty was Robert Stevenson, born in Glasgow in 1772.

His mother remarried the tinsmith, lamp maker and mechanic Thomas Smith following the death of Stevenson's father when Robert was only an infant.

An engineer with the Northern Lighthouse Board, Smith later took on his stepson as his assistant, and this was a career in which Stevenson excelled.

Aged only 19, he was responsible for supervising the erection of a lighthouse on the island of Little Cumbrae, in the Clyde, while in 1797 he was appointed engineer for the Northern Lighthouse Board in succession to his father – a post in which he served for 50 years.

Responsible for the design, construction and improvement of 15 lighthouses in his lifetime, including those of Bell Rock, in the Orkneys, Mull of Galloway and Lismore, Stevenson was also responsible for a number of other civil engineering projects that included the Regent Bridge and London Road approaches to Edinburgh from the east and the Hutcheson Bridge in Glasgow.

Elected a member of the prestigious scientific think-tank known as the Royal Society in 1815, the ingenious engineer died in 1850, while Stevenson College, founded in Edinburgh in 1970, is named in his honour.

Three of his sons – David, Alan and Thomas and a number of their sons – followed in his footsteps by also becoming famous lighthouse designers.

Alan Stevenson, his eldest son, who was born in 1807 in Edinburgh and who died in 1865, was also employed for a time with the Northern Lighthouse Board and was responsible for the construction of 13 lighthouses around Scotland between 1843 and 1853, including those of Cromarty, and Ardnamurchan Point.

His brother David, born in 1815 and who died in 1886, was the civil engineer who designed more than 30 lighthouses around Scotland, including those of Whalsay Skerries, Fladda and Turnberry, while his son, David Alan Stevenson, born in Edinburgh in 1854, built a number of lighthouses that included those of Fidra, Stroma and Tor Ness before his death in 1936.

David Stevenson's other son, Charles Stevenson, who was born in 1855 and died in 1950, built more than 20 lighthouses between 1887 and 1937, including those of Skroo, on the Fair Isle, Flannan Isles and Duncansby Head.

The youngest son of Robert Stevenson, Thomas Stevenson was the civil engineer who was born in 1818 and died in 1887.

The designer of lighthouses that included those of Muckle Flugga, St Abb's Head and Turnberry Point, he was also the inventor of a scientific device known as the Stevenson Screen, used by meteorologists.

Married to Margaret Balfour, Thomas Stevenson is also famous as the father of one of

Scotland's greatest literary figures – none other than Robert Lewis Balfour Stevenson, better known to posterity as the poet, essayist, travel writer and novelist Robert Louis Stevenson.

Aged only 44 when he died, Stevenson was nevertheless responsible for a great body of work that endures to this day.

Born in Edinburgh in 1850, his father, while encouraging him with his early writing ambitions, still had his son marked out for a career in engineering.

It was in order to satisfy his father that Stevenson enrolled as an engineering student at Edinburgh University in 1867 – but soon dropped out after adopting a bohemian lifestyle and becoming a regular visitor to some of the capital's more disreputable haunts.

Honing his writing skills along the way, he later buckled to pressure from his father to seek a more stable career and enrolled as a law student at Edinburgh University.

His studies were intermittent, but Stevenson still managed to qualify for the Scottish Bar in 1875 – but he never practised law, embarking instead on a journey through France that resulted in the publication in 1878 of his *An Inland Voyage*.

It was in France that Stevenson met the American Fanny Vandergrift Osbourne, whom he later married, and, with his wife and stepson Lloyd Osbourne in tow, he set off on further travels throughout the world – mainly in search of a climate that would be beneficial to his weak constitution.

Travels with a Donkey in the Cévennes was published in 1879, followed by the 1883 *The Silverado Squatters* and *Treasure Island*, with *The Strange Case of Dr Jekyll and Mr Hyde* and *Kidnapped* both published three years later.

In 1890, he and his wife and stepson finally settled on an estate in the village of Vailima, on the Samoan island of Upolu, and became known to the native islanders as Tusitala – meaning Teller of Tales.

He died only four years later, and was buried by the natives on Upolu's Mount Vaea, on a spot overlooking the sea.

Inscribed on his grave is the 'requiem' that Stevenson himself penned and the last two famous lines of which are:

> *Home is the sailor, home from the sea,*
> *And the hunter home from the hill.*

Continuing the literary tradition, his cousin D.E. Stevenson was the Scottish author of romantic

novels who was also known by her married name of
Dorothy Emily Peploe.

Born in 1892, the author wrote a series of
novels, based mainly in the Scottish Borders, and
which include the 1923 *Peter West*, the 1959 *Still
Glides the Stream* and, three years before her death in
1973, *House of the Deer*.

Another cousin, Robert Alan Mowbray
Stevenson, born in Edinburgh in 1847 and who died
in 1900, was the Scottish art critic who wrote for the
Pall Mall Gazette and held the post of professor of
fine arts at University College, Liverpool.

Returning from the world of the pen and
back to the world of engineering, George Stephenson,
born in 1781 at Wylam, near Newcastle, and his son
Robert, born in 1803, were noted English engineers
and locomotive designers.

They built the *Locomotion* for the Stockton
and Darlington Railway in 1825, the first locomotive
for a public railway, followed four years later by the
famous *Rocket*, capable of what was then considered
the astonishing speed of 30mph.

Across the Atlantic, Adlai Ewing Stevenson,
known as Adlai E. Stevenson I, was the 'father' of a
famous American dynasty of the name.

Born in 1835 in Christian County, Kentucky, his great grandfather had immigrated to the United States from Ulster – having settled there after moving from his birthplace of Roxburgh, in the Scottish Borders.

Adlai Stevenson later settled in Illinois, where he became a leading Democrat Party politician – serving as congressman for the state, Assistant Postmaster General of the United States in 1885, and 23rd Vice President of the United States, under Grover Cleveland, from 1893 to 1897.

He died in 1914, but the Stevenson political tradition was carried on through his grandson Adlai Ewing Stevenson II, born in 1900, who served as U.S. Ambassador to the United Nations from 1961 to 1965.

In both 1952 and 1956, he was the unsuccessful Democratic candidate for the Presidency.

Renowned for his quick wit, it was during one of his Presidential campaigns that he was assured by a supporter that he was certain to get the vote of "every thinking man in the U.S." – to which he dryly replied: "Thank you, but I need a majority."

He died in 1965.

A great grandson of Adlai Stevenson I, Adlai

Stevenson III, meanwhile served as U.S. Senator for Illinois from 1970 to 1981.

Yet another of his descendants, McLean Stevenson, born in 1927 in Normal, Illinois, and who died in 1996, chose a rather different career path, that of acting, and becoming best known for his role as Lt. Colonel Henry Blake on the popular television sitcom *M*A*S*H*.

In commerce, Dr John Stevenson was the merchant, developer and medical practitioner of Scots-Irish descent who was born in 1718 and died in 1785.

He immigrated to America from Ulster in 1734 along with his brother Henry, who was also a doctor, settling in what was then the rather sleepy trading city of Baltimore, in Maryland.

Stevenson is considered today to have laid the foundations of the port of Baltimore's wealth, by exporting wheat and flour to Ireland, while his brother established the city's first smallpox hospital.

Chapter four:

On the world stage

While bearers of the Stevenson name and its variations have excelled in such diverse fields as civil engineering, literature, politics and commerce, they have also gained distinction through a wide range of other endeavours.

Behind the camera lens, **Robert Stevenson** was the English film director and screenwriter who was born in 1905 in Buxton, Derbyshire.

Moving to California after the end of the Second World War, he later went on to direct an impressive total of nineteen films for Walt Disney, including the 1964 musical *Mary Poppins*, starring Julie Andrews, and for which he received an Oscar nomination for Best Director.

Other Disney films include the 1959 *Darby O'Gill and the Little People*, the 1965 *That Darn Cat!* and, from 1974, *Herbie Rides Again*.

Stevenson, who prior to settling full-time in the United States directed the 1937 *King Solomon's Mines*, died in 1986.

Born in 1949 in Takapuna, New Zealand,

Pamela Stephenson is the actress and comedian whose film roles include the 1983 *Superman III*.

She first came to the attention of the viewing public through her roles in the popular 1980's British television comedy sketch show *Not the Nine O'Clock News* – where she first met the Scottish comedian and actor Billy Connolly, whom she married in 1989.

A lady of many talents, she is also a clinical psychologist and author of the best-selling 2002 *Billy* and the 2003 *Bravemouth: Living with Billy Connolly*.

Going back in time to the era of silent films, **Charles Stevenson** was the American actor born in 1887 in Sacramento, California, and who died in 1943.

The star of more than 100 films between 1914 and 1925, his credits include the 1916 *Luke, the Candy Cut-up* and, from 1920, *High and Dizzy*.

In contemporary times, **Jessica Stevenson** is the English actress and writer also known by her married name of Jessica Hynes.

Born in London in 1972, she was one of the creators of the 1999 British television sitcom *Spaced*, while she has also appeared in other popular sitcoms that include *The Royle Family*.

Also on the stage, **Nicola Stephenson**, born in 1971 in Oldham, Lancashire is the English actress best known for her roles in a range of British television soaps, sitcoms and dramas that include *Brookside*, *Clocking Off* and *Holby City*.

Across the Atlantic, **Bob Stephenson** is the American actor, born in 1967 in California, whose television roles include that of Sheriff Jimmy Taylor in the *Jericho* series, and whose film credits include the 1997 *Con Air*, the 2006 *School for Scoundrels* and the 2007 *Zodiac*.

No television or film actor can perform on screen without a script, and one leading scriptwriter is the former English newspaper journalist **John Stevenson**. Born in 1937, he is a regular writer for the popular British television soap *Coronation Street*, while in the 1980s, along with fellow *Coronation Street* scriptwriter Julian Roach, he wrote the comedy drama *Brass*.

In the highly competitive world of sport, **Alexandra Stevenson** is the top American tennis player who, as a junior, took the U.S. Open Girls Doubles title in 1997. Born in 1980 in La Jolla, California, one of her professional career highs was reaching the semi-finals of Wimbledom in 1999, making her the first female qualifier to do so.

In the boxing ring, **Teofilo Stevenson** is the

former amateur heavyweight boxer who was born in 1952 in Camagüry, Cuba.

Along with fellow Cuban Felix Savon and the Hungarian Lásló Papp, he is one of only three boxers to win three Olympic gold medals – taking gold in heavyweight at the 1972, 1976 and 1980 Olympics.

On both the cricket pitch and the fields of European football, **Bob Stephenson**, born in 1942 in Derby, is the former multi-talented English sportsman who played football for Derby County, Shrewsbury Town and Rochdale throughout the 1960s and first-class cricket for Derbyshire between 1967 and 1980.

In athletics, Toby Stevenson, better known by his nickname of **Crash Stevenson**, is the American pole vaulter born in 1976 in Odessa, Texas, who won a gold medal at the 2003 Pan American Games, silver at the 2004 Olympics and gold in the same year at the U.S. Indoor.

Generations of bearers of the Stevenson and Stephenson names have also distinguished themselves on the bloody field of battle.

Born in 1817 in Fredericksburg, Virginia, **Carter Stevenson** was the army general who fought for the Confederate cause during the American Civil War of 1861 to 1865.

The general, who survived the war and died in 1888, is buried in the Confederate cemetery in Fredericksburg and commemorated in the form of a marble bust in the Vicksburg National Military Park.

Fighting on the opposite side to Carter Stevenson during the war was **John D. Stevenson**, born in 1821 and who died in 1897.

A practising lawyer in Franklin County, Missouri, and a member of the Missouri State Legislature before the outbreak of the war, he went on to become commander of the 3rd Brigade, 3rd Division, XVII Corps of the Union Army – better known as the famed Irish Brigade.

In a much later conflict his namesake, **John Stevenson**, was the U.S. Air Force general who served in both North Africa and Europe during the Second World War.

The general, who was born in 1914 and died in 1995, was shot down and captured by the Germans in August of 1943, but survived to become, between 1967 and 1971, an administrator for the space agency NASA – serving as director of mission operations in the Office of Manned Space Flight.

Considered to have been one of the inspirations for Ian Fleming's fictional spy character

James Bond, **Sir William Stephenson** was the real
life spymaster who played a key role in Allied
intelligence during the Second World War.

Born in 1897 in Winnipeg, Canada, to an
Icelandic mother and a father who hailed from the
Orkney Islands, his birth name was William Stanger –
but he assumed 'Stephenson' as his surname after
being adopted at an early age by a couple of that name.

Granted a commission with the Royal Flying
Corps during the First World War, he earned both the
Military Cross and Distinguished Flying Cross, while
after the conflict he went on to become a wealthy
businessman.

His international business and social contacts
proved valuable in gaining him vital inside
information on Hitler's Third Reich, and in June of
1940 he was selected by the great British wartime
leader Winston Churchill to run the secret British
Security Co-ordination (BSC), based in New York.

Known by his intelligence codename of
Intrepid, he was also responsible for setting up Camp
X, in Whitby, Ontario, where Allied intelligence
operatives were trained.

Knighted in 1945 for his wartime services
and made a Companion of the Order of Canada in

1979, the spymaster, who died in 1989, was portrayed by David Niven in the 1979 television series *A Man Called Intrepid*, based on Stephenson's best-selling book of that name.

From the field of battle to the creative world of music, **Ronald Stevenson** is the pianist and composer who was born in 1928 in Blackburn, Lancashire, to a Scottish father and an English mother.

Now resident in Scotland, his many compositions for orchestra include his 1965 *Scots Dance Toccata* and the 1976 *Young Scotland Suite*.

Across the Atlantic, **Tommy Stevenson**, nicknamed "Steve", was the American jazz trumpet player who was born in 1914 and who died in 1944; known as a 'high note' trumpeter, he played for top bandleaders who included Blanche Calloway, Cootie Williams and Don Redman.

In a different musical genre, **Sir John Stevenson** was the Irish composer who was born in Dublin in 1761 to an Irish mother and a Scottish father.

Knighted in 1802, he is best known for the publication, along with the poet Thomas Moore, of *Irish Melodies*, while in 1814 he became the first organist and musical director of Dublin Castle's Chapel Royal.

The composer, who died in 1833, was also

responsible for a number of haunting airs that include *Ladies of our Lovely Isle* and *Buds of Roses*.

From haunting airs to hauntings of a rather different kind, **Ian Stevenson** was the Canadian biochemist and professor of psychiatry who was a firm believer in reincarnation – defined by him as the survival of personality after death.

Born in 1918 in Montreal, he studied medicine at St Andrews University, in his father's native Scotland, and also at Montreal's McGill University.

His fascination with the paranormal in general and reincarnation in particular, led to his appointment as head of the division of perceptual studies at the University of Virginia – and it was here that he left behind an eerie legacy.

Some years before his death in 2007, he bought a cabinet, placed it in a room in the university, and sealed it with the use of a special combination lock based on a series of letters and numbers.

He told colleagues that he would attempt to 'communicate' the combination to them after his death, perhaps in the form of a dream, and thereby prove the concept of reincarnation.

The cabinet – at least at the time of writing – remains locked.